John Morris

The last Illness of His Eminence Cardinal Wiseman

John Morris

The last Illness of His Eminence Cardinal Wiseman

ISBN/EAN: 9783337059286

Printed in Europe, USA, Canada, Australia, Japan

Cover: Foto ©ninafisch / pixelio.de

More available books at **www.hansebooks.com**

THE LAST ILLNESS

OF

HIS EMINENCE CARDINAL WISEMAN.

BY

JOHN MORRIS,

CANON PENITENTIARY OF WESTMINSTER.

In fide et lenitate ipsius sanctum fecit illum. *Ecclus.* xlv. 4.

LONDON:

BURNS, LAMBERT, AND OATES,

17 Portman Street and 63 Paternoster Row.

1865.

PIETATI . ET . CLEMENTIAE . DIVINAE

COMMENDA

SANCTISQUE . SACRIFICIIS . ADJUVA

ANIMAM

CHARISSIMI . IN . CHRISTO . PATRIS . NOSTRI

EMINENTISSIMI . ET . REVERENDISSIMI . DOMINI

NICOLAI

TIT . S . PUDENTIANAE . S . R . E . PRESB . CARD

ARCHIEPISCOPI . WESTMONASTERIENSIS

QUI . PLACIDISSIME . OBDORMIVIT . IN . DOMINO

JAMDIU . SUSPIRATO

DIE . XV . FEBRUARII . MDCCCLXV

VALE . MAGNE . PRAESUL

IN . VITA . NOBILIS

NOBILISSIME . IN . MORTE

APUD . DEUM . MEMENTO . NOSTRI

ET . ECCLESIAE . VIDUATAE . SPONSAE . TUAE

CARDINAL WISEMAN'S LAST ILLNESS.

THE impression made upon my mind by the few weeks of the Cardinal's last illness, I cannot hope to convey to others; but the example of virtue of which I was a witness was so striking, that I think it my duty towards the memory of one whom I greatly love and venerate, to place this narrative within reach of more than those to whom I can relate it by word of mouth. The Cardinal was in so especial a way the property of Catholics, wherever they are found, that I consider that they have a right to be informed of the grand and holy ending of his useful life; and for this reason, after much thought, I have come to the conclusion that I might publish, and ought to publish, even those things that I heard from him in confidence relating to himself. This I now feel, looking back upon his illness, that if I could tell it exactly as it happened, I should do him the fullest justice, and render the greatest number partakers in the privilege that was enjoyed by a favoured few. There was not a word uttered by him all through

that time that any one could wish to hide, or that
could fail to excite edification and affectionate ad-
miration, though much less, I regret to think, when
read in a narrative such as this, than when heard
uttered in the plaintive low tone that his weakness
caused him to use.

I do not know when to date back for the com-
mencement of the Cardinal's last illness. On Sunday the 15th of January he suddenly sunk so low
that he was in imminent danger of death for many
hours. But though this complete exhaustion was
most unexpected, he had been very far from well for
some time before, and his state of health had been
such as seriously to alarm his experienced medical
advisers. A wound had, apparently spontaneously,
opened in his right foot, which resulted in mortification. The doctors had enjoined upon him
complete rest and quiet, and had required that he
should be treated as a man whom sickness prevented
from attending to his work. Those who knew the
Cardinal can form an idea of the irksomeness of con-
finement to his ever-active nature and fertile brain.
It was very difficult for others to appreciate the in-
jury that he was doing to himself when he allowed
them to bring their cares or their anxieties to him
for his ready sympathy, or when they asked his as-
sistance in those duties of his pastoral office, in which
he took such delight, but which now overtaxed his
failing strength.

By the kindness of my good friend Mr. Charles

Hawkins, whose surgical skill and tender care have for so long been of inestimable service to the Cardinal, I am able to give in a note a short account of the progress of his fatal disease.* I can thus put my imperfect knowledge on one side, and confine myself to that which we who were about him saw and felt.

I confess that for some time past my mind had

---

* For the last twelve years the Cardinal has been more or less under medical treatment. In 1853 he was found to be suffering from diabetes. In 1854, before he left Golden Square, Dr. Robert Fergusson, Dr. Nairne, Mr. Tegart sen., and Mr. Charles Hawkins met in consultation, and an unfavourable opinion of the case was formed. In July 1856 His Eminence received great benefit from the Baths of Vichy ; and, in the following year, he went through a course of the Vichy waters at Leyton. In October 1859 he was seriously ill, and on that occasion Dr. Todd was consulted. He was suffering from irritability of the heart and a weakened state of circulation, with great prostration. The diabetes was then increasing. He left for Rome at the beginning of December 1859. While there he had an inflammation of the veins of the right leg and an affection of the lungs, accompanied by great debility. The diabetes was then very bad. An operation was performed on a carbuncle on the back on the 23d of June 1860. The Cardinal left Rome on the 11th of August, and on the 17th Mr. Hawkins operated on another carbuncle at Paris. On the 21st he returned to England, and in about six weeks the carbuncle was well. At Christmas he was again in a feeble state. In 1862 the veins of the right leg were affected. In 1863 the swelling returned, and showed some symptoms of mortification. The Cardinal suffered much in August 1864 from want of sleep and affection of the eyes, and during the whole year there was great debility. On the 26th of November, which was the last day he was at Leyton, two blisters appeared on the right foot; and on the 8th of December there were signs of mortification. By the 11th of January the foot was quite well ; and on the 12th erysipelas attacked the face.

been full of vague misgivings that he was not to be with us much longer. In September last he placed in my hands the Ms. of the verses then just written, which he subsequently printed for private circulation, under the title of a " Retrospect of Many Years." As soon as I read them I felt a sinking of heart, and an impression that the end was probably not far off. His mind had gone back to the days of his boyhood, and he was reviewing his career, and connecting together the early days with later times. Respecting one stanza, in which he spoke of those being few who sympathised with him, I remonstrated with him, begging him to omit it as very far from true; but he shook his head with a smile. When, however, later he was confined to his sofa, and amused himself by sending copies of these verses to his friends, he was much gratified by the affectionate remonstrances that that stanza drew from all. Great as his courage was, and unchanging his determination to struggle on from a sheer sense of duty, sympathy was particularly welcome to his affectionate heart.

I could not help noticing, when I accompanied him in his drives, as I frequently had the happiness of doing before his grave illness, that on every occasion he said something that showed how much his thoughts were fixed on death. Some allusion to it there was sure to be; not as from a man who expected soon to die, but as from one to whom the thought of death was very familiar. But he would speak most readily of early times. Some of the things

he used to say raised very high my opinion of the great
purity and simplicity of his life, and quite prepared
me for what he said to me afterwards, when the sha-
dow of death was upon him. He had evidently for
some years past, ever since the greatness of his danger at Rome, made a very careful survey of his whole
life, and the habit of introspection, both intellectual
and moral, grew upon him latterly. I recollect his
saying on one of these occasions that he went to Mr.
Hawkins, now many years ago, and said to him, "I
have got *diabetes;* I am sure that I have, from my
increasing irritability."

Twice he went through with me, in these drives,
what he was going to say, or had said, at the Sainte
Union Convent at Highgate, on St. Nicholas's Day.
I am very sorry to think that I did not go with him to
hear his last sermon. He had thought much about
it, and was pleased with the thoughts respecting St.
Nicholas that dwelt in his mind. He looked upon
him, he said, as a connecting link not only between
the East and the West, but between days of perse-
cution and of peace. "Can you imagine any thing
grander than the Fathers of the Council of Nice rising to receive a Bishop who had been in prison as a
Confessor of the Faith, and had been the friend and
companion of Martyrs? What should we think of the
appearance amongst us of one of our priests who had
narrowly escaped martyrdom under Elizabeth?" A
pretty little flower-vase stood on the Cardinal's table
during his illness, bearing the inscription "*La Sainte*

Union reconnaissante. Dec. 6, 1864." It often held the flowers that Mrs. Howard of Corby was so kind as to send, not knowing that she was to precede to a better life the Cardinal, to whom she was so full of kindness and attention.

The feast of his Patron Saint brought to His Eminence a large number of personal letters of congratulation and good wishes. These he devoted the next day to answer. The exertion of his little function at Highgate on the 6th, and spending the 7th at his table, writing thirty or forty letters, had a very bad effect on the wound in his foot, which began to show symptoms of mortification. He had intended to have been present at the High Mass at Farm Street on the 8th, the Immaculate Conception; and a little later, to have re-opened the chapel in the Marylebone Road; but he was obliged to excuse himself from both engagements.

Though now for a considerable time confined to his sofa, he was yet able to receive many who called to see him. As it was difficult for him to write, he dictated many letters, and amused himself by looking over the little dramas which he had written for children. In the last of these, *The Witch of Rosenberg,* he was much interested. It was written for St. Leo's Convent, Carlow, the Superioress of which has lost in him a cousin. Mr. G. C. Stanfield sketched a scene for him, Mr. James Doyle drew the costumes, and Mr. Molloy set the songs to music; and when I came into his room one day, I found him superintending with great satisfaction the packing of all these treasures, with his own perfectly clean and un-corrected Ms., in a little box, which two Sisters of Mercy, who had called on him, were decorating with gold paper and lace, as a Christmas surprise for the convent children.

On the 13th of December, a meeting of the Bishops was held in London. The Cardinal was well enough to preside at their deliberations, though still kept by the doctors on his sofa. One of the Bishops has told me that he took advantage of an interval in the grave deliberations of that day to say that he wished to inform the Bishops that he had made a complete provision for his successor of every thing that was necessary for the decorous discharge of his episcopal duties; but that, thinking that these things were all of a sacred character, he had desired to leave him some secular memorial, and that he had had a centre-piece for his table executed in Rome by Brugo, which was to be used on that day for the first time. This group was placed but on one other occa-sion on the table before him who had given the idea which is here so admirably carried out. Our Divine Lord is giving the keys to St. Peter, who stretches forth his veiled hands to receive them; St. John is standing by with a lamb in his arms, and sheep and lambs are browsing around on the hillock, which a palm-tree surmounts. The following inscription on the base is from the Cardinal's pen. He printed it on a card, intended to show his guests their places

at his table, with a translation, which is also sub-
joined.

Inscription on the Group of O. L. and St. Peter.

QVI·CHRISTI·POST·ME·PASCIS·ME·DIGNIOR·AGNOS
IPSO·IN·SYMPOSIO·SIS·MEMOR·OFFICII
NEC·DVM·TE·LAVTE·TRACTAS·SOCIOSQVE·BEATOS
LAZARVS·ANTE·FORES·LANGVEAT·ESVRIENS

N. C. W.

Translation.

WHO, AFTER ME, MORE WORTHILY, OF CHRIST DOST FEED THE SHEEP,
REMEMBRANCE OF THY DUTY, EVEN AT THE BANQUET, KEEP.
NOR WHEN, FOR THEE, WITH GENIAL FRIENDS, THE FESTIVE BOARD IS SPREAD,
LET LAZARUS, BEFORE THY DOOR, SINK FAINT, FROM WANT OF BREAD.

N. C. W.

The Cardinal had been invited, some time before
this, to give a lecture at the Royal Institution. The
subject chosen by him was "Shakespeare," and the
lecture was to have been delivered on the 27th of
January. In this undertaking he took the liveliest
interest. He determined to dictate beforehand all
that he was going to say, and to have it ready in
print when the lecture was given. With this in-
tention, he asked the Rev. Dr. Clifford, the chaplain
of the Hospital of St. John and St. Elizabeth, to be
his amanuensis; and this was his last intellectual
work. Though suffering greatly at the time from
weakness of the eyes, he read through all the books
that he could collect respecting Shakespeare, and he
was particularly interested by the fact that lawyers
claimed Shakespeare as a lawyer, and doctors as a
doctor, from the special knowledge shown by him on
those subjects. He amused himself by asking all his
friends for their definition of "genius." I remember

hearing him say that he considered it to lie, after the facility of becoming great in any art or science, in an instinctive appreciation of all things that in any way bear upon it, and in the power of using all such collateral helps accurately and happily. His idea was that Shakespeare did not derive his accuracy of description of various mental states from observation, but from "introspection." In this the Cardinal was only describing, though perhaps unconsciously, his own mental practice; for few men probably have exercised a more habitual self-analysis, or a more independent self-judgment; and it was but natural that he should feel a sympathy with the quality of mind that was so remarkable in himself—the almost intuitive perception of every thing that could be brought to bear from any side in illustration and support of his own beloved science.

On Wednesday the 11th of January the Cardinal went out of doors for the last time, taking a drive in Battersea Park, and there probably he caught a cold in his face. On the 12th, for two hours and a half, he dictated his Shakespeare lecture to Dr. Clifford. He directed me to write a letter of sympathy and encouragement to Father Charles Bowden, of the Oratory.* He signed this

---

* Father Charles Bowden has been so kind as to place the letter at my disposal.

"8 *York Place, W., Jan.* 12*th,* 1865.

"DEAR FATHER CHARLES BOWDEN,—Although not able to write myself, I cannot longer refrain from expressing to you my

letter, which was the last that bore his signature. The next day he wrote his initials to the *Imprimatur* of a little book that the Servite Sisters of Bond Street, Chelsea, had prepared for publication. On Friday the 13th Dr. Clifford was otherwise engaged, so that the Shakespeare made no progress, which the Cardinal much regretted, though he acknowledged that perhaps it was better for him, as he felt ill and little fit for work. He told me that he saw clearly before him all that he proposed to say; that he meant to write it very fully for publication, and compress as much as possible in the delivery.

Saturday came, and he managed to dictate a few pages of Shakespeare, though feeling very weak and ill. At the end, Dr. Clifford tells me that he said smilingly to him, "*Eh, basta così*, we shall soon get over our work. We have got the beginning and the end. It will not require much more for completion. I have in my mind every sentence I am going to dictate of this lecture. So it is only a question of

---

great satisfaction at the happy result of the painful trial to which you were subjected in the case of the girl M'Dermot. I sincerely congratulate you upon it, and hope you will not be discouraged in doing good by the hard and unjust treatment which it sometimes may bring upon you. I can only say that, if any thing, you were too lenient and sparing of others in your vindication of yourself. This, however, only enhances your merits; and I trust that God will fully requite you for what you have done, and draw from what you have suffered greater good than probably you can have anticipated.

"With my blessing, I remain

"Yours affectionately in Christ,

"N. CARD. WISEMAN."

a few days now, and a little freedom from other business. If I can't deliver it myself, there will be abundance of matter for somebody to read in my stead." I went down with him about two o'clock from his bedroom to the drawing-room, where his luncheon had been brought, and sat with him, talking to him. He could eat nothing; and I hear that in the evening he could not take any food. About five Dr. Clifford left him, at his request, that he might try to sleep, as the night before had been restless. When he got to the door, the Cardinal called to him, " Now remember, you are not to preach at Warwick Street to-morrow. I shall want you early."

Earlier in the afternoon, the Cardinal expressed a hope that he might be able to say Mass on Sunday. Dr. Clifford told him that he thought it was impossible, as he seemed so ill, and his eye was so bad. He seemed to cling to hope, and remarked, " I must say Mass—and then, there is poor Heneage." Dr. Clifford suggested that he might ask Father Richards, of the Oblates of St. Charles, to say Mass for him. He hesitated for some time, and then said, " Very well, just ask Father Richards to have the goodness to come at seven to-morrow morning. I will go to Communion instead of saying Mass." The last Mass that he said was on the previous Thursday.

For a fortnight or more before, he had had as a neighbour, in his dressing-room, his great friend, the Rev. H. P. Heneage, who was confined by illness to his bed. This Saturday evening, for the first time, the Cardinal sent him word that he was not well enough to sit with him as he usually did, but that he must go at once to bed. About three o'clock in the morning he rang for his servant, and found it necessary to break his fast. Later in the morning, about half-past ten o'clock, he went into Mr. Heneage's room, and sat with him some time, seemingly much better, speaking with his usual voice, and conversing with interest on current events. He expressed to Mr. Heneage his gratification at the manner in which the proposal to present a testimonial to him on his jubilee was put forward in the *Weekly Register* of that day. When Dr. Clifford came, according to his promise, he found him in Mr. Heneage's room. In answer to his inquiries, he said that he had passed a very bad night, had had to call up Roper, his servant; that he had been very sick, and had in consequence not been able to go to Communion, nor even to go into the chapel. He had heard Mass, as well as he could, from his own room. He then, somewhat suddenly, told Dr. Clifford to follow him into his bedroom. He appeared to be concerned about something. He sat down and said, "Do you know, Clifford, such a strange thing happened to me after you left yesterday. Soon after you went away, I fell into a heavy, restless sleep on the sofa. I can't say how long it lasted. On awaking from it, I could not make out where I was. I tried to arouse myself, but could not. I had a dim recollection of having been for some time previously engaged upon *some* work, but what it was, I could not remember. I knew that some one had been helping me, but I could not think who it was. I could not even think of Shakespeare's name. This lasted, I should say, about an hour. My mind was a perfect blank. That is very strange, isn't it? I never experienced any thing like that in my life before."

He then took his rosary out of the pocket which hung by the chair, and began to say it. Dr. Clifford bathed his eye, and suggested that, as he was so weak and had had no food, he should take some tea, or a glass of wine. He could not, he said; he felt low, but could take nothing. He frequently asked what time it was, and remarked that it seemed very long. "Only twelve o'clock! How slowly the time passes!" About twelve Dr. Clifford and Roper his servant left the room, at his request. Dr. Clifford then went into Mr. Heneage's room, and determined to wait there, to be ready to go to him in case he moved. In about an hour he went in to him again, and found him still in the same position, and almost in a stupor. "What a famous talk you have been having!" he said, after some little while. He then uttered one or two incoherent sentences, and Dr. Clifford, rather alarmed, tried to induce him to take some stimulant. He made a feeble effort to take the glass, but could not. Dr. Clifford then helped him to take some sherry; but after having just tasted it, he shook his head, to intimate that he could take no more.

Between two and three Mr. Charles Hawkins came, and he then said that he was very ill, that he was not able to eat any thing, and that he could not imagine why he had not sent for Mr. Hawkins when he felt so poorly overnight. A medical man had once told him that as long as he continued to be able to eat, he would do well; and this had made a considerable impression upon him, and loss of appetite always alarmed him. Mr. Hawkins caused him to go to bed, and ordered him strong stimulants. Returning about six, he found that the Cardinal hardly knew him; and about nine, when Dr. Munk and Mr. Edward Tegart also came, His Eminence had fallen into a state of unconsciousness, from which he could only be aroused for a moment by being spoken to in a very brisk, clear voice. It was not at any time, Mr. Hawkins tells me, a state of coma, but simply exhaustion; the languid circulation not carrying sufficient blood to the brain to enable it to perform its vital functions. The unconsciousness continued to deepen; so that when, at half-past ten, Dr. Hearn made every effort to arouse him, when about to administer Extreme Unction, the sole effect produced was a personal recognition of Dr. Hearn, but without the power to attend to what he said or did. The next morning he asked, " Is Dr. Hearn in the house? And what did he do to me ?"

Mr. Hawkins at once sent for the Reverend Mother of the Hospital, and she remained as the Cardinal's nurse for the month during which his powerful constitution gradually gave way. More perfect nursing than hers I suppose there never was. A noiseless step, a gentle hand, a steady, audible voice, but rarely and never unnecessarily heard, a most watchful eye, great endurance of fatigue, and the conviction that in a sick-room nothing is trifling, are qualifications conferred as a natural gift with the taste for nursing, and improved by long practice, as well in the hospitals at Scutari as in the wards of Great Ormond Street; but there was added the devotedness of a Religious engaged in her especial vocation, and, as Dr. Manning well called it, the " singular reverence" of a daughter engaged in her labour of love. All the Cardinal's friends owe her a deep debt of gratitude; and I know not how it can be paid, unless it be by rendering still more efficient the admirable charity of the Catholic hospital, in which the Cardinal has always taken so great an interest.

A great amount of stimulants, administered at short intervals by Mr. Hawkins, who remained with him all night, preserved the Cardinal's life over the immediate danger of death. In the morning he was very feeble, but quite himself. His first thought showed his usual consideration for others. He urged Reverend Mother and Roper to go to bed, saying that he did not deserve that so much trouble should be taken about him, and thinking that they had been with him for days. He said, "I have seen Mr. Hawkins several times." Reverend Mother answered, "Yes, he has been with you every hour."

"Is it only one night?" he asked; "I thought it was a week or two. I must tell Mr. Hawkins to go to bed. He must not lose his rest for me." In a way that was very characteristic of him, he noticed much more the effect of the weakness on his mind than on his body. He told me, as I knelt by his bedside on Monday morning, how he felt his inability to string his thoughts together. After his professional visit in the afternoon, Dr. Munk told him, in accordance with a promise exacted by him when dangerously ill at Ushaw in 1859, that his danger had been very grave, and that he had received Extreme Unction in the night. When so told, he made but little remark, as his way was, simply saying that he was quite unaware of what was done. But it dwelt much on his mind, and produced a sense of the nearness of death that did not seem to lessen with any apparent improvement. The impression was all the greater, for, as he then told me, serious as his previous illnesses had been, it had never been thought necessary to administer the last Sacraments to him.

In talking with him about it, on Tuesday morning, I asked him whether if he were to be again in serious danger, there was any one he would wish to be sent for. He said, "No one but Dr. Melia," his confessor. And then after a little silence, he said, "I suppose it was not God's Will that I should go. Perhaps my work was not yet done." I answered, "Ah, my lord, you must be like St. Martin, *qui nec mori timuit, nec vivere recusavit.*" I saw his face light up as the familiar words corresponded with his own thought.

After an interval, he added, "I have been thinking much of that saying of St. Augustine, that 'no one, however free his conscience may pronounce him of sin, should depart this life without penance;' and it makes a great impression upon me, coming as it does from a *saint.* I hope God will take my illness as a part of my penance. But I confess to you that I find it far easier to make an Act of Love than an Act of Contrition, for God knows that I have never deliberately offended against Him."

It was this expression of his that I meant was so distinctly borne out by the details he had given me of his early life, into which of course I cannot enter; but I may add a similar expression used by him in Confession to a penitent of his, who said that it was a very difficult thing to make an Act of Contrition; when he, interpreting the phrase by his own mind, replied: "Yes it is, for one cannot recollect that one's will has ever gone against God."

"I have never cared for anything," he said, "but the Church. My sole delight has been in everything connected with her. As people in the world would go to a ball for their recreation, so I have enjoyed a great function."

He added, "What a curious thing it is, that I should have been anointed when in a state of unconsciousness! I have made it a practice all my life to pray every evening that I might retain my

senses to the last.   But I suppose it does not make
much difference."   However, the end was not yet
come, and when it did come, the prayer was fully
heard.

This afternoon a telegram was sent in the name
of Dr. Hearn, the Cardinal's Vicar-General, to Mgr.
Talbot at the Vatican, that he might tell the Holy
Father that the Cardinal, though now better, had been
in extreme danger, and beg him to send him his
Apostolic Benediction, in case the danger should re-
cur.   The Cardinal was very much pleased when he
was told of it, and most highly prized the blessing
which a telegraphic message from Mgr. Talbot on
Wednesday conveyed to him.   A few days later he
telegraphed his warm thanks to the Holy Father,
saying, at the same time, that he was gradually im-
proving.

He told me then that it was the Roman etiquette
that when a Cardinal was in danger of death, a priest
should be sent to the Vatican in his carriage, with its
usual two footmen, as though the Cardinal were himself there : and he said that he had had a curious
instance in his own case of the way in which the
Romans noticed such things; for the rumour spread
about Rome that he was dying and had sent for the
last Blessing, for they had seen Dr. Manning driven
up to the Vatican in his carriage, as he happened to
have an audience with the Holy Father one day immediately after he had been out for a drive with him.

On Tuesday the 17th he was evidently better;

and I do not know that there was any other day through that long month on which we allowed ourselves to entertain much hope. He sat up awhile in his chair, and spoke so cheerfully and so like himself, that if it had not been for the erysipelas in the face, which was then fully out, we might have thought it impossible that he should have been so seriously ill. His right eye was swollen and quite closed, and it was with great difficulty that he was able to open it during the next fortnight. He probably never used it again. A painful sore formed in the inner corner, which never healed; and he began now to ask that the inflammation might be bathed with icy-cold water. This was the only thing that gave him any relief; and during the whole month, almost night and day, kneeling at his bedside, Reverend Mother performed this office for him, when not occupied in her other nursing duties. It was the only thing he asked for all through his illness, except now and then for a little iced water to drink. He would ask for it sometimes with quiet playfulness, sometimes almost plaintively, but never querulously. Once he said: "Reverend Mother, please bathe my eye, or your eye, or somebody's eye, whose-ever it is, for I am sure it does not feel like mine."

On this Tuesday he said to me—and he told the story with his own minuteness and accuracy—"I remember when I had a villa at Albano, Mgr. Ferrari, the Prefect of the Pope's Master of Ceremonies, who had been sent to the Palace at Castel Gandolfo by

the Pope, for a change of air after a very severe illness, called on me, and said: *Ah! Eminentissimo,
abbiamo bussato alla porta, si, ma non ci siamo ancora
entrati.* 'We have knocked at the door, but we have
not been let in yet.'"

Dr. Clifford has been so kind as to give me the
following account of the next morning. "On Wednesday, 18th January, the Cardinal wished me to
read him some portions from the New Testament.
He took the Bible I had brought upstairs, and, after
some time, pointed out to me the thirteenth chapter
of St. John's Gospel. The task of finding out the
place must have been very trying, as even then he
could not use one of his eyes, and the other was very
weak indeed. He told me to read slowly; and it
seemed to me that while I read from the thirteenth
to the end of the sixteenth chapter, he was meditating
most intently.

"Perhaps I ought to say that, on going into the
room, he asked me if there was any news. To this
question I replied in the negative, lest I should fatigue him too much. 'What!' His Eminence answered, 'nothing in the papers about the French
Bishops?' I then told him that they continued to
protest against the Circular of the Government for-
bidding the Encyclical to be read by the Bishops to
their people, and that, notwithstanding the prohibi-
tion, one or two had read it openly from the pulpit.
At this he seemed very much pleased, and said: 'I
am very glad the French Bishops are standing out so

bravely for the liberties of the Church. That will console the Holy Father very much.'

"When speaking of the Encyclical, I think he said that he hoped to say something on it. 'The French Bishops have spoken,' he said; 'but as yet I've said nothing.'"

On Thursday morning, about four o'clock, I carried the Blessed Sacrament into the Cardinal's room, and gave him Communion. He was certainly the worse in health during the following day. The medical men, therefore, found it necessary to say that he must not think of going to Communion for the present. After this he communicated but once until he received in form of Viaticum. It was this deprivation that led him to say to Reverend Mother the words quoted by Dr. Manning in his funeral sermon: "They little know of what they are depriving me. A little fasting would tire me less than this longing." And at another time, "O, how much longer am I to have patience? How long am I to wait? They are keeping me from my only consolation."

Day now went by after day, for the next fortnight, each so like the other that it is impossible to keep them apart in one's mind. I saw but little of the Cardinal during this period of his illness. Three or four times in the day I would go to his ante-room and learn from Reverend Mother, or from his indefatigable servants, Newman or Roper, how he was going on; but, as the doctors particularly wished him to be as little disturbed as possible, and as, besides,

he was often asleep when I was there, I but seldom
spoke to him. For my own consolation I jot down
what I remember of the things he said on those
occasions.

Once he said, "Have you ever heard Dr. Melia's
story of the two old Mexican Jesuit Fathers? They
were exiles, and lived at the Noviceship on Monte
Cavallo. Every day they were to be seen along the
road leading to the Porta Pia, taking their walk *a
ventidue ore*, and they were as well known there as
the gate itself. At last the younger of the two fell
ill; and the other, Father Herrera, who was ten years
his senior, and his confessor, attended upon him with
all assiduity and tenderness. After his illness had
lasted a good while, one day Father Herrera said to
him: '*Padre mio*, it is time for you to go into your
agony.' 'No, not yet,' is Father Eligio's answer;
'go and sleep; there is full time for you to have a
rest, and Brother Grassi shall call you when I want
you.' After an interval Father Eligio says, '*Fratel
Grassi, datemi una buona cioccolata*,—Give me a good
cup of chocolate;' and then, when he had taken it,
'*Adesso, lasciatemi per un' ora buona*,—Leave me now
for a good hour.' At the end of the time he sent for
Father Herrera, '*Adesso si, padre mio, che mi metto
in agonia*,—Now I am ready to go into my agony;'
and so he died."

The story struck me very much when the Cardinal
told it, and still more it strikes me now that I have
written it down. Though it was told with his usual

sense of humour, it tells to me, especially now, a tale of earnest. I have since seen his own calm, fearless looking upon death; his own forecast, so to speak, of the manner in which he should die; and when he told us to leave him alone for a good space of time, especially before and after Communion, we used to say to one another that he reminded us of Father Eligio.

I cannot recollect how the conversation came round at another time to the examinations in the Roman Schools, but I remember his saying, that in one concorso in his favourite subject, the Scripture, he had written a full paper, which, by some accident, had been mislaid, and the class-list had been made out without his name, when some of the professors said (as he gave it), " Surely So-and-so has written ;" when his paper was looked for and found, and the whole list was moved down a place; that of *Præstantissimus solus*, with the gold medal, being assigned to him.

One afternoon he said to me, " I am sure it would do me more good to have a long talk about Monte Porzio than to be kept so much alone." I answered, " Well, let's have a good talk about Monte Porzio ;" and then he straightway flung himself into it. " I can see the colour of the chestnut-trees, and Camaldoli, and the top of Tusculum. What a beautiful view it is from our Refectory window! A new-comer does not value Monte Porzio properly. It takes a hard year's work in Rome to enable you to appreciate it. I loved it dearly. I keep a picture of it in my

bedroom, both here and at Leyton. They have kept ·
the Rector's chair in the place where I used to sit. I
got that gold chair for Pope Leo's reception, and I
always used it afterwards. I used to sit there writing
for hours after every one was in bed, and then I
would refresh myself by a look out of the open window into the moonlight night."

There was one immense consolation that God was
pleased to give to the Cardinal during his last illness.
He had insisted that the first Mass said by the Rev.
Richard Waldo Sibthorp, after his long absence of
twenty years from the altar, should be celebrated in
his private chapel. When that Mass was said, on
the Feast of the Conversion of St. Paul, the Cardinal
was too ill to see Mr. Sibthorp, but his gratification
at the good news was heartfelt.

On that day, the 25th, Mr. Heneage returned to
the Convent of the Good Shepherd at Hammersmith,
of which he is the Chaplain. He saw the Cardinal
before he left, and went away thinking him to be
much better. He did not know that in a few hours'
time the surgeon's knife was to operate on a small
carbuncle that had formed in the right eyebrow.

The courage with which he bore these most painful operations was heroic. He uttered no sound, he
did not even wince, and no one could have formed an
idea of the severity of the pain. When in Rome, as
the very fearful wound produced by the operation on
his back was being dressed with caustic (a proceeding
that, I have heard Mr. Hawkins say, must have been

as painful day by day as the original operation), he heard one day the Italian surgeons say to one another, " *Ma non sente,*—He does not feel."

In telling me of it afterwards, just before he was taken ill, he said, "I could assure them that there was no fear of mortification on the score of my not feeling the pain." He wrote of it thus, at the time:

" *Rome,* 30*th June* 1860.

"It is a week to-day since I underwent a terrible operation. Two cuts were made in the form of the Cross on my back, each the length of this paper, the four flaps then dissected under (like a muffin) and a large piece cut out of the inside. It was for a most malignant carbuncle; and the operation was quite successful, and I have no doubt brilliant. I will not say what I suffered, but our good God strengthened me to bear it without complaint. The doctors said it must have been awful pain; but I tried to take my Cross in the spirit of a better one, and, thank God, succeeded. For a few days all was doubtful, till the tumour got fairly circumscribed and isolated by caustic, which has been freely applied, so that the dressings have sometimes recalled to me the operation. My strength has not given way. I have regained my appetite; every thing looks favourable, and to-morrow Mr. Hawkins arrives. The tumour is coming away, and if nothing new occurs, I may hope in God and our Blessed Lady to be convalescent. Pray,

therefore, to Almighty God for me, and thank Him
for all His goodness, especially for having made me
suffer so acutely with His Blessed Son, and for having
given me strength. My blessing to ——. God bless
you and ——. This is the first letter I write, and
the only one to England. What a scrawl!"

He bore pain so well, that it was difficult to believe that there was so much pain to bear; but when
all operations were over, and there was nothing left
for us but to wait at his bedside for the death that
came so slowly, the tender-hearted surgeon, whose
steady, skilful hand had so often prolonged his life
by these very operations, said, as he looked at him,
"Ah, we never acknowledged how much pain he had
to bear." In Rome, while undergoing all this pain,
he held in his hand the little silver crucifix from his
portable altar, the same that so many saw in his
hands when they were closed in death.

No one who saw him take his medicine would
have formed any idea that it was distasteful. It
was extremely bitter, and he never lost the taste
of it day or night. Once before he was taken
seriously ill, when the remark was made that it must
be very disagreeable, he said, "No; on the contrary,
I am very glad of it. Is it not well to have something to suffer? I have not any real pain with my
foot, and so I am very glad to have this little cross."
Afterwards he said that whatever he eat or drank
had the same taste, and that he liked to have a

perpetual offering to make. "It is not worse than gall."

Reverend Mother has given me the following interesting note of a conversation with him on his endurance of pain:

"The night of the 26th January, the Cardinal said something about the operation, and told me to pray he might be patient. I said he was patient, and that his courage and patience were both wonderful. 'I am so glad you think I bear pain well. I was always considered such a coward about pain. I believe I feel less than others, and make more fuss.' I said I thought it was the other way. 'When I was young they always told me I was a coward: do you think some people feel pain more than others?' I said yes, I felt sure of it. 'I have asked doctors, and all don't agree. As there are different degrees of muscular strength, I think there might be of sensitiveness in the nerves; but perhaps it is that some are braver than others.' I said, as to talking of pain and showing it, I thought a good deal depended on what one was taught as a child. 'Yes, I know a great deal is in one's own power. I have always tried to fight against my cowardice. Many years ago I determined never to call any thing pain, or mention it till it was unendurable; and I am very glad you think I bear pain well, for you must see so much suffering.' I said, 'You bore the operation beautifully, and surely you had great pain before, though you did not complain.' 'Well, not bad pain,—only weight and a dull

burning feel, as I had before that carbuncle in Rome.'
'That must have been dreadful.' 'It was sharp enough.
When I knew it was to be done, I sat on the chair,
with my hands over the back, and laid my head on
them. I couldn't help giving two great gasps; but
Monsignor Manning, who was outside, never heard
any thing. You know they cut so deep,' and then
he gave one of his smiles; 'they thought I was so
quiet they could not have done enough, and there
must be more to cut.' 'The dressings were worse,
weren't they?' 'The dressings were worse than the
operation,—harder to bear. They burnt away, and
thought there was mortification because I kept quiet.'
'Why didn't you tell them how it pained you?' 'Oh,
it only made a little more to suffer, and it was better
to have it done thoroughly. I did not want to turn
coward again.' "

I do not remember to have heard any details of
this portion of the Cardinal's illness. It was impossible for us who saw how great an amount of nourish-
ment and stimulant was daily administered to him by
the directions of the medical men, and who saw no
corresponding increase of strength, or any thing more
than a very partial and temporary rally, not to have
our hearts fail us as we looked at the future. The
change for the worse was so gradual, that it could not
be seen between day and day, and better or worse rest
at night naturally produced corresponding variations
of strength. Though, therefore, there was probably
not one of us who, by the beginning of February, re-

tained much hope for his life, still it came upon us suddenly when he himself was the first to speak plainly about his state.

On the evening of the Purification, Thursday the 2d of February, he asked Reverend Mother how he really was. She answered, "You do not gain strength." "What do the doctors say of me?" "They told me there was a possibility of recovery, if your strength could be kept up." "Tell me what you really think of my state." She said, "I do not believe you will recover. I know it is possible, but nothing seems to do you any good, and you sink every day." Then he said, "I feel myself that I am sinking and losing strength. I will ask the doctors to-morrow how I really am."

During the night he was conscious of a loss of control over his mind. It alarmed him, as any symptom relating to the brain ever did, and it strengthened his determination to ask the doctors how he really was. Accordingly, when Mr. Hawkins and Mr. Tegart came in the morning he said to them, "I will ask you to go into the next room and consider what you have to say to me, for I have a question to put to you." When they were gone, seeing Mgr. Searle by his side, he said to him, "Won't you go in with them?" He answered, "No, your Eminence, I am never present at the doctors' consultations, and indeed it is not necessary, for I have already told them all that I have to say." The Cardinal replied, "I am glad of that, for I want them to know every thing."

When they came in again, he said to them, "I have felt what it was in the night to be subject to illusions. I had the strength to know that they were illusions, and to put them away; but I feel that the time might come when I should not have this strength. I therefore want you to tell me exactly how I am." Mr. Hawkins answered, "Your Eminence, if it were only your face, there would be nothing in that for us to be afraid of. What really is serious is that you do not rally or gain any strength. You remember that when I performed that operation on you in Paris, you rallied so fast that in four days you were able to cross the Channel. But now, though so many more days have elapsed, you have not gathered any strength." "Is there any thing that you can do to me to give me strength?" On hearing that every thing had already been done that their knowledge suggested, he said, "Thank you, I understand."

Then after a pause he said, "I have a few temporal matters to arrange—thank God, very few; shall I be safe in leaving them for a day or two?" Mr. Tegart's reply was, "Your Eminence was never clearer in your life than you have shown yourself to be in the account you have just given us of your feelings during the night. Why not use that clearness for any thing you may have to do? If you grow weaker, you will certainly not get clearer." "Thank you," he said again, "I understand."

After a pause, he said that he should like to be taken downstairs to the drawing-room that day; and

Mr. Hawkins promised to order a proper chair to be
sent, and to come himself to see him moved. He said,
"Leave the chapel-door open, that I may look in as
I pass, for perhaps I shall not see it again."

Instead of looking into his chapel through the
open door, he was taken into it on his way downstairs.
He remained for a few minutes before the Blessed
Sacrament, all around him kneeling; and then the
chair was turned for him to face the image of the
Blessed Virgin, a beautiful marble bust by Benzoni,
which he had brought from Rome, as an *ex voto* for
his recovery there in 1860. He was then carried
down to the drawing-room, where the bed had been
placed against the middle window, facing the folding-
doors. I believe that he expressed his wish to be
moved, because he thought that the larger room would
be so much more convenient on such an occasion as re-
ceiving the Chapter, and again, for the Office of the
Dead after his decease. My belief is that he thought
beforehand of every thing, and that he arranged the
proper place and time of each thing in his own mind.

When the doctors had left him, and Reverend
Mother had returned, he said to her, "Well, did you
hear what they said?" She answered, "No, father;
but I can guess." "They tell me I am going home.
Is it not nice?" "For you," she said, "but not for
us." "Oh, it is so nice: it is like going home for
the holidays after working hard at school. Do not
you know the feeling of going home? I am going
to be with my Father. I am going to rest;—no more

work, no more troubles, no more scoldings, all peace.
I am just like a child going home to rest and be with
its Father."

In the evening I had been out to give Benediction, and when I returned I was told that he had
asked for Dr. Hearn and myself. Dr. Hearn tells
me that on this occasion he asked him to take care
that, if there was any sermon at his funeral, it might
be preached by his friend Dr. Manning. When I
went into the room, I found him sitting in his arm-
chair. It was a rest to him to be moved occasionally
to the chair from his bed. "Oh, I am so glad you
are come," he said; "come close to me. I am like a
child going home from school for the holidays. This
has been a most eventful day for me. I felt last
night that I must not think of the health of my body,
but of my soul." And then he told me what had
passed between himself and the doctors in the morning, as I have given it above, except that in relating
it he twice said "London" by mistake for "Paris."
He then went on with, "Now I have a question I
wish to ask of you. How often do you think I may
receive in the form of Viaticum?" I so little under-
stood that it was a question that he was putting to
me for solution that I did not answer. On which he
looked up in his old, sharp way, and said quite quickly,
"What was that you settled awhile ago about one of
your nuns?" Then I knew that he was speaking to
me, for I had consulted him about a month before on
this very point, telling him what St. Alphonsus said,

and asking him whether in his judgment I was right in the course I was pursuing. I answered him accordingly: "In my opinion, your Eminence is perfectly justified in communicating under the form of Viaticum every day." "Ah," he said, "that was the conclusion I came to in Rome." After a long pause I said to him, "Did you not very much enjoy your little visit to the Blessed Sacrament on your way down stairs to-day?" He answered, "Oh yes, and my Madonna, and my relics, and all lit up too." After a little while he assented, when I asked, "Your Eminence proposes to receive the Holy Communion to-night?" Then I said, "Shall I put the things ready?" "No," he answered, "be quiet." And then, "Is Monsignor Searle in the house?" "Yes, he is upstairs." "I think he would like to give it me," he added, and most tenderly and affectionately it was said. I then saw that when I had offered to put the table ready, he had thought that I meant to bring him the Holy Communion; but indeed it was very far from me, now or ever during this sad time, to be unmindful of the prior claims of one who for five-and-twenty years has been in so intimate a relation to him, and whose personal loss in his death is far greater than that of any of us. It must be no light consolation to him to remember that the dying Cardinal said to him, "Certainly, if ever I am where I am able, I will be with you."

This day, Friday the 3d of February, was to us the beginning of the last stage of the Cardinal's illness. We could not now hide from ourselves the imminence of our danger, and every little word began to assume a tenfold value in our eyes. Happily for me, I was now admitted into the circle of his nurses, on whom the succession of sleepless nights was beginning to tell. A portable altar was brought into the ante-room, and when the folding-doors were opened, he could see the priest at the altar from his bed. Here, with the exception of the Sundays, I said my Mass, to my great consolation.

After his professional interview on Saturday, Dr. Munk returned to the Cardinal, at his own request, and then told him of his approaching death, and that his state was so precarious that it was impossible to answer for his life for twenty-four hours.

In the evening of the same day, while hearing Confessions, for which duty I had most reluctantly left the house, I received a message that he wanted me, and that he was to be waked when I came. Reverend Mother tells me that he said to her, " Let me be waked if any body comes whom I ought to see. Sleep now does me no good, so it is only waste of time."

I was alone with him for a long while. He began by telling me he had settled his temporal affairs · with Mr. Harting that day; " and now," he said, " I shall have no more anxiety on this side." He spoke about his funeral, saying, as quietly and unconcernedly as if it had been some function he was himself about to perform, " I shall look to you and Patterson for the ceremonial. See that every thing is done quite right. Do not let a rubric be broken." After some other details he added, "And, of course, the religious will say the office here in the room."

And so they did,—representatives of eleven religious orders of men, including the Congregations of Secular Priests, but, according to Roman etiquette, not including the Fathers of the Society of Jesus: and of those eleven orders, all, if I am not mistaken, received from him the work in the diocese in which they are engaged; and very nearly all were introduced into London by him.

From the beginning of his more serious illness in January, the prayer for him had been inserted in the Mass. At first it was the prayer which is said on the Bishop's Anniversary-days; but this was soon changed, at his request, to the prayer for the sick, which he made me read over to him, to see whether it was the one that he remembered to have said in Rome during the illness of one of the Popes. He now thought that the time was come when the other, and more urgent prayer, for "a sick man near to death" should be substituted for it. He also requested that the Chapter should be summoned for the next day, to receive his solemn profession of faith. As it was past post-time on Saturday evening, these notices were sent by hand, and special messengers went down by night to enable Canons Weathers and Last, who lived the furthest off, to be present. He also requested me to telegraph to Rome to Dr. Manning to

return at once. "Whom will you send it to?" he
said. I answered that Dr. Manning's address was in
the *Via del Tritone*, as before. He replied, "Better go
to head-quarters. Send it to Mgr. Talbot. He will
be able to tell the Holy Father how I am."

He rehearsed to me what he intended to say to
the Canons on the following day, and told me that
he did so to enable me to follow him more readily,
and to jot down, as far as possible, his very words.
I will give them as I wrote them down immediately
afterwards, and as each one who heard them remem-
bers them to have been spoken, in their proper place
in my record of the Sunday. This I am permitted
to do by the Chapter to whom they were addressed.

From these subjects he went on to speak more
of himself. " I do not wish any one to read to me
when I am dying," he said; "but I had rather be
left to my own meditations." I remarked, "But you
would like to have the Litany, my lord?" "What,
the 'Commendation of a Departing Soul,' the Church's
words," he answered, quite brightening up. "I want
to have every thing the Church gives me, down to
the Holy Water. Do not leave out any thing. I
want every thing."

On Friday, and again on Saturday, the Cardinal
received the Holy Viaticum. He passed, I think I
may say in consequence, a quieter night on Friday,
and on Saturday there was not much change for the
worse. On Sunday, however, he seemed much weaker
than on the previous day.

In the morning he received the Holy Communion in the Mass which was celebrated in his ante-room by Monsignor Searle. The Count de Torre Diaz served that Mass; and after it the Cardinal took an affectionate farewell of him, encouraging him to continue his zealous interest in every thing good and Catholic.

At about three o'clock in the afternoon of Sunday the 5th of February, the Canons assembled at his house. The only two members of the Chapter who were absent were Dr. Manning, the Provost, who was in Rome, and Canon Shepherd, at Bermuda.

On the previous evening the Cardinal had spoken to me of his desire to receive the Sacrament of Extreme Unction a second time. His own feeling was, that he had sufficiently rallied from the pressing danger in which he was first anointed, to constitute this a new danger. When he mooted it to me, I said to him, " Well, my lord, as this is a question of fact, had we not better refer it to the doctors ?" " Yes, you. can ask them," he said. "And shall we go by what they say?" " Oh, I don't see that at all," he answered; " it's our business, and not theirs."

He was vested, as he lay in bed, by Mgr. Searle, who had so often vested him before. He had on his rochet, his red mozzetta and zucchetto, his pectoral cross and gold stole; and he wore the sapphire ring which, when he was made a Cardinal, he received from the College of the Propaganda, in return for the offering which it is their privilege to receive from

all newly-created members of the Sacred College. I
said to him, "Canon Hunt, as the Missionary Rector,
will anoint your Eminence." He bowed his head. I
added, "And will you have the *Asperges* from the
Senior Canon?" He answered, looking round at me,
"I want every thing."

The Canons then came into the room, wearing
their choir dress, and formed a semicircle around
him, on his left side. Mr. Patterson was there, as
his Master of Ceremonies. He had previously requested Mgr. Searle to assist him on his right hand;
and he told me to be on his left, and to read the Profession of Faith for him. The large picture of Pope
Pius IX., which all who have been in his drawing-
room will remember, looked down upon us, and seemed
to form part of the group, who were engaged in one
of the most solemn acts the Church has devised. The
Archiepiscopal Cross was placed at the foot of the
bed; and there it remained for the days of his life
that were yet left.

Canon Maguire, as the Senior Canon, in the absence of the Provost, having sprinkled the Cardinal
with holy water, I knelt by his side and read the
Creed of Pope Pius IV. When it was ended, the
book of the Gospels was handed to him to kiss, for
the oath with which it concludes. He put his hand
upon it, and said, "Put it down." And then, "I wish
to express before the Chapter that I have not, and
never have had in my whole life, the very slightest
doubt or hesitation of any one of the Articles of this

Faith; I have always endeavoured to teach it; and I transmit it intact to my successor."

The Missal was then lifted up to him, and he kissed it, saying, " *Sic me Deus adjuvet et haec Sancta Dei Evangelia.*" He then added, "I now wish to receive Extreme Unction at your hands, as the seal of my Profession of Faith."

· Canon Hunt then took off his Canon's mozzetta, and put on a surplice and stole. The Cardinal knew, and had remarked long before, that Canons ought not to administer the Sacraments in their choir dress; and he evidently saw this little observance of rule with satisfaction. If he had recovered sufficiently, I doubt not that he would have made some remark upon it.

When he had received Extreme Unction, he said, in so low a tone of voice that I doubt whether any one save myself, who was kneeling close to him, heard every word, "Having now received from you what the Church has to give, I have a few words to address to you. I fear that I cannot speak loud enough for you all to hear, but one or two of you will hear me, and will tell what I say to the others.

"I feel that the time has come when I am about to resign into the hands of Almighty God the care of the Diocese that I have so long administered. I wish you to understand that I have not myself interfered, nor have any who are about me, or who have spoken in my name, ever interfered with that order for making provision which God has constituted here. It is left to the appointment of the Holy See, and to that system of election which I strove hard to establish, and to which it is now intrusted. I am very anxious for the good of the Diocese; and you will choose that name that you consider most fit and worthy to fill this high office.

"I have one word to say, and it is to beg you to cherish peace, and charity, and unity, even though it may be at the price of our occasionally having to give up our own individual opinions for the sake of peace. And if in the past there has been any thing that has made against charity and unity, in God's name let it pass into oblivion; let us put aside all jealousies, and let us forgive one another and love one another.

"I know that I have not been worthy to succeed to the great Bishops whom you have had, and I have not promoted piety towards God and to His Blessed Mother, and devotion to the Holy Eucharist, as I should have done; and I have not edified you by my personal piety. I ask God to forgive me; I beg of you to forgive me; and I beg of you to pray for forgiveness for me."

Then in a very faint voice he began *Sit nomen Domini benedictum*, and gave his Pontifical Blessing. Afterwards each Canon, in his rank, came up to him, and kissed him on both cheeks, and withdrew.

The medical men were able to say, in the evening, that he had borne this strain upon his little stock of strength better than could have been hoped for. I think that the Canons, accustomed as they are to see dying persons, left him with a better hope, from his appearance, than they had entertained before they saw him. He had not at all the appearance of a dying man; but his countenance continued florid until just before his death. Mr. Herbert, who saw him when asleep only two or three days before he died, said that he should have thought from his appearance that he might recover.

That same Sunday evening another painful operation was requisite. For some time before he left his bedroom, a large carbuncle had formed on the right temple. Mr. Hawkins had tried, if possible, to prevent its growth by burning it with caustic; but the use of the knife became necessary; and in the evening, after he had received the Chapter, it was opened with three cross cuts, in the form of a star. There had been two cuts in each former operation, the third was therefore unexpected, but he only very slightly winced. Dangerous as it was, the knife passing the arteries of the temple within the distance of the thickness of the paper on which I write, and though he was so weak that not a drop of blood could be spared, the operation was quite necessary, as the doctors said, in order "to give him a chance." To Mr. Hawkins he said, "What you think it right to do, it is my duty to submit to. Remember that." His remark to the medical men, when the time came, was "I am in your hands; do with me as you like."

In the night after this operation, the Cardinal

called Reverend Mother to him, and said, "How do
I come to be here?" She thought he meant in that
room, and answered, "You came down on Friday."
"I mean how do I come to be here? They promised
me I should be in Heaven to-night." She said, "They
are trying to keep you with us a little longer. It is
very selfish, but we want you a little longer." And
then he said very low, as if he did not wish any one
to hear, "Do you know I could not help thinking,
while they were cutting me, that it was very unkind.
to try to keep me out of Heaven. I had been hoping
all day that I should go home to-night." Afterwards
he said, "Will this make me well?" Reverend Mother
answered that it was the only chance. "If I do recover at all, shall I be fit for work? Because if not,
I shall be only in the way." She said that she sup-
posed that if he got better he would be fit for work,
but not for a long time. "I do not think I shall get
better. I feel my strength going out of me, and nothing does me any good." And then he said something about being disappointed, but that he must have
patience. "Pray that I may be patient."

Monday the 6th was a day of considerable exhaustion. I can only find a record of a single sentence uttered by him. It was this, "My mind is now
quite clear, and I only wish to go home as soon as
God pleases." In the night he said to me, "*Nondum
statim finis*. How long am I to wait?" I answered,
"Ah, my lord, you have many long hours of patience
before you yet." "Do you think so?" he said.

On the 7th, I find that I wrote of him that he
was not only not worse, but certainly better,—by
which I meant brighter, and that he took some food
more readily. The wound in the temple looked more
healthy, and the swelling in the face was reduced to
some extent, though the right eye remained closed;
his voice, too, was certainly clearer, which told of a
clearer throat. But there were other symptoms that
were unfavourable. It seems wonderful to me now
how I could have said of this day, and again of the
9th, that I had a tiny ray of hope. One felt at the
time how foolish it was, and yet it was impossible to
prevent one's spirits rising with any little change for
the better. He was perplexed at his own rallying,
and from time to time doubts came over him as to
whether he was really dying. Sometimes he would
say that if God meant him to live a little longer, he
would be glad for the sake of the work. He did his
best to live, saying once that if he could add a week
to his life he was bound to do so: but the thought
that was the deepest and most prevalent during the
last twelve days was the wish to die.

Just before he was taken ill, a new marble altar
for his private chapel arrived from Rome. Unfor-
tunately it was broken on the voyage; and from
this cause he never saw it in its proper place. His
bedroom was so near to the chapel that it could not
be erected while he was lying ill; but when he was
carried downstairs, he expressed to Monsignor Searle
his wish that it might be put up, saying, "If any

thing happens, it will be done; and if I get better, it
will serve as a thank-offering."

He was quietness itself, and his patience and
obedience were perfect. He had not said a queru-
lous word during the three weeks he had been so ill,
and he was ever ready with gentle thanks for any
little service. He passed whole days in silence, ut-
tering only a very few sentences; but all the while
he was quite recollected and himself. He seemed to
us like a man who was calmly meditating, and he
occasionally gave us a glimpse of the subjects that
were occupying his mind. Some of them are shown
in the two conversations I subsequently had with
him, which I have yet to record. But I was most
touched when I heard him whisper to himself, thinking aloud, "He showed no mercy to Himself." His
obedience was very striking: he would move immediately exactly as he was told; and it was a
touching sight to see him, when so weak that he
could hardly swallow, obeying like a child what Mr.
Tegart told him to do, in that voice of quiet authority
that doctors of body and soul are alike obliged at
times to use. A day or two before this, when we
were giving him some food, he said, "I do this from
pure obedience, for it does me no good." But we
never once saw him dejected or in low spirits. Once
I was giving him a mixture that must have been
very disagreeable,—strong beef-tea with brandy in
it,—but I thought that he had ceased to be able to
distinguish one thing from another. To my great

amusement he said, "That is what I call dull—beef and brandy." I laughed; and he said, "What's that?" Dr. Hearn, who was leaning over the head of his bed, said, "You set him off by something you said." "That was American," he answered; meaning, I suppose, the use of the word "dull."

About half-past five in the morning of Thursday the 9th, he said, "Reverend Mother, take hold of my hand. I want you to promise that you will obey me." "Yes," she said, she would. "Promise to tell me whatever I tell you to tell me, whether you like it or not;" with something more about obedience that Reverend Mother could not catch. "I wish to die as an act of simple obedience, and I desire you to tell me to die. But first ask me, Do you desire to be dissolved and to be with Christ? And I shall say, Yes. Do you desire nothing on earth but the enjoyment of God? When I say Yes to that, you are to say, If you desire nothing more on earth, go to God. Now say it. I wish my death to be an act of pure obedience." Then Reverend Mother put the first question to him; and he answered "Yes;" and she broke down in the middle of the second. In about five minutes he said, "You did not do what I told you, or I should not be here now. Where's Canon Morris?"

I was sleeping on the sofa at his feet, when Reverend Mother called me. He said, "I wish to die out of pure obedience. *Cupio dissolvi et esse cum Christo.* Could you tell me to die?" I answered,

" You must wish to die when God wills, and to live
as long as God wills." " Yes," he. said, " that is what
I wish; but *melius est mori et esse cum Christo;*"
and I shall never forget the plaintive touching tone
in which the last words were uttered. I rejoined,
" You will get all the merit of the obedience. Shall
I tell you to wish to live as long as God chooses, and
to die when He chooses?" He said, " Yes." " Then
I bid you wish to live as long as God wills, and to
die when He wills." After a pause, I added, " Will
you say, Give me here my Purgatory; in this sense,
that you wish to be with Christ, and have to wait?"
He answered, "I will, I do. I say it from all my
heart. That is just what I say."

Then, with long pauses, he went on thus: " Is
this a prophetic calm?" . . . "I think a good many
will be sorry for me." " I know some who will," I
answered. " Protestants, I mean," he continued;
" I don't think they will always think me such a
monster." This led him to the thought of his intended lecture; but he only said, " Give my blessing
to Dr. Clifford. He was very kind in helping me.
He will miss me." . . . "I hope they won't cut up
my papers much. I think I have left a good many
papers that will do good. You and Manning* will
see to them. I hope they won't want much cutting
up. There are some papers from my boyhood. I
hope they may be found useful."

---

* The Cardinal's literary executors are the Right Rev. Provost
Manning, D.D., and the Very Rev. Canon Thompson.

. When I asked him for his blessing for Reverend Mother, who never spoke to him unnecessarily, but who was very anxious to get his blessing before he died, he said, "God bless you, Reverend Mother. God bless you,"—making the sign of the cross over her,—"and reward you for all you have done for me. Persevere to the end."

I said, "When you see God, will you think of us?" He answered, "I will try to think of all then. But oh! what am I? I am unworthy even to think of God. What have I done for God?"

I suggested to him that he should use his clearness of mind to make the Acts of Faith, Hope, Charity, and Contrition. He said, "I will. Make them for me out loud, slowly and distinctly."

I did so in the fewest possible words. He then said, "I charge you, dear Canon Morris, as a notary of the Roman Catholic Church, to record what I have just done in a solemn document, and to sign it in my name, to be kept always in the archives of the Church of Westminster; and say that I die in the faith and Communion of the Roman Catholic Church; and add to it that I have never doubted or wavered, and have always had those Acts in my heart that I have made with my dying lips. Add it to that more solemn Act I made,"—referring to his Profession of Faith before the Chapter. "Do you accept my commission, and do you remember all I have said?" I answered, "I remember every line of it, and will do all you have told me."

He went on after a while: "There is one thing that is a mortification to me. I should have liked to have had my people about me with tapers at the last; but in this country I suppose I must give it up." I said: "Oh, you shall have them about you." "Do you remember the glorious death of that Bishop—a Benedictine, an exile from Spain—who was dying all alone, when a whole colony of his people, going, I think, to Australia—Benedictine monks in their habits —knelt all around him with their tapers?" I said, "See how God answers prayers, even in things like these."

He said, "I want every body to know that on this, which will be probably the last day of my life, my mind is quite clear. I think God sent me the last two days to prepare me for to-day." Finding him so clear, I asked him for a matrimonial dispensation, which he gave.

"What sort of a report will the doctors make when they come?" I answered: "They will say your mind is clearer, but your body weaker." "Do you think I am weaker? What is my pulse like?" I said, "It is very quiet." "Is not quiet, strength?"

"If I recover, I will tell you some curious mental phenomena which have never been before observed."

"How shall I die?" I answered: "You will grow weaker, and then fall asleep, and when you wake you will see our Divine Lord." "Why will they say that?" "Because you have been sinking so steadily."

During the night, whenever he woke he wandered;

but even his wanderings were edifying. At one time he spoke about unity ; at another, he must get out of bed, that he might make sure he was doing his duty. His first collected words on Friday morning were to ask for the Holy Communion. This gave him a beautiful opportunity of showing how implicit his obedience was. When told that the doctors would be here in a few minutes, would he wait, he acquiesced at once, and had his stole taken off : and when they had gone, I asked him whether he would receive Communion then, and he said that it depended upon us. Monsignor Searle gave him the Holy Viaticum, and this was the last time that he received Communion. He had previously received the Holy Viaticum on Tuesday and Wednesday. On one occasion, I do not now remember when, but I think it was on Thursday, he asked whether recourse had been had to any supernatural means to obtain his recovery. On being told that we should not think of applying any relic to him without his knowledge and consent, he said, "That is right. I have never done so in life, and I do not mean to do so in death." For himself he would not look for any extraordinary favour.

On Friday the 10th, after a silent morning, at a quarter to one he called me by name. I answered, and knelt by him. He said, "God bless you. I cannot tell you from one another. You seem to me to be all of one heart in one body, striving to do your duty."

At a quarter-past two Dr. Hearn heard him say,
"Many things I have still to expiate. . . . .
It is the failing of strength; there is no use in
mystery. . . . . I shall retire to rest, until God
sends for me."

At five he asked for his Rosary, and to be left
quiet for a time.

In the evening, at a quarter-past nine, he called
me, and I knelt down beside him, having first lifted
him towards me, as he wished. He said: "Is there
any one in the room?" I answered, "No one but
Reverend Mother," and then, "and she is gone now."
"Are you only in the room?" I said, "Yes, nobody
is here but I."

·He waited I should think five minutes to rest, and
then put his arm on my shoulder and said: "I have
every reason to be grateful to Our Blessed Lord. I
cannot tell you the joy I feel in my affection for Our
Divine Lord, and my gratitude is not less. I have
gone on always making those Acts. I wish to be
in perfect conformity with Our Blessed Lord, and I
only want to fulfil His holy will. My mind has been
constantly dwelling on what it is to be with God. I
wish I could tell you what it has appeared to me to
be: quite different from what I thought it in life.
But I fear I never shall be able to tell you." I said,
"You will tell us what you thought when we meet
you in heaven." "Oh, there will be something
grander there!" I said, "We shall find heaven
grander and more noble than our grandest thoughts

of it." He answered, "To think—fifty million times
—and then multiplied again and again."

He then asked me about his strength, and could
he reckon on the strength of his body from the power
of his mind: and he said, "We cannot weigh the
strength of our body by drachms. I wish I could
describe to you the curious sensations of the loss of
physical strength."

"Who would live an instant?"—I thought he
said, 'Lift me up an instant:'—he repeated, "Who
would live a moment?"—and paused. I said, "If he
could be in heaven." He said, "Yes, if he could be
in heaven. Oh, how stupidly strong I have been; it
has kept me from heaven. We must be dissolved to
be with Christ; but I am far from that yet. This
strength keeps me from heaven."

I asked him, "Are you always thinking of God?"
He answered, "Oh, of course!"

A little later in the evening he was moved into
his chair, and Reverend Mother was bathing his eye,
while I was kneeling by him. He made an effort to
tell us his meditation on heaven, but he was tired, and
the right words would not come. He said, "Do not
think I am wandering, for I am not." And he was
not, but only some sentences were audible, and it was
clear that his memory did not serve him with the
words that would express his thoughts. I heard some
such sentences as "diamonds, and on every facet a
Virgin or a Martyr." And then the two striking
phrases, "Rush through the angels into God;" and

after a time, during which he had evidently been
pondering on the eternity of the Beatific Vision,
"I never heard of any one being tired of the
stars."

On Saturday the 11th, Reverend Mother went
home to her Convent for a few hours. Before she
left, he said to her, "What shall you tell the Sisters
about me—that I am dead?" "No, you are not
dead yet." "Yes, I am, I am dead." She laughed,
and he laughed too, and said, "Of course, I am not
dead in one way, or I should not want Roper to shave
me; but I am dead to the world. I am as completely
separated from creatures, and as alone, as if I were
dead. Tell them to pray for me that I may die."
When Reverend Mother returned he did not remark
it for a long time, and then he said, "Is that our
usual Reverend Mother?"

This day, when told what numberless prayers were
being offered for him, and that every one wanted his
blessing, he said: "You need not ask for it, for I
give it with all my heart to those who are so kind
and show so much interest and affection. I am not
worthy of it." To Dr. Melia he said, "*Benedico non
solo lei, ma tutta la diocesi*,—I bless not you only,
but all the diocese."

It was during this afternoon that the last operation was performed. Dropsy in the right eyelid was
caused by the erysipelas, and the pressure on the eye
was so great that it was necessary to cut across it.
The relief from the operation was evident, but the

wounds from all these incisions remained very terrible to the last.

Reverend Mother has been so good as to give me this note of this evening. "About half-past eight the Cardinal called me, and said something about flowers and candles which I could not catch. He then asked the time, morning or evening? Soon after he said, 'This dying is very curious.' Then he asked why the room was so dark. When the Blessed Sacrament was brought into a place, there should be lighted candles. 'It does not signify being evening; I am not obliged to say Mass or communicate during Mass. I can receive at any hour.' 'Shall I call Canon Morris?' 'Yes, Morris knows I did not receive this morning. In five minutes I shall be ready; you get the room ready.' I can't go upstairs, but my God will come to me. It will be like a sudden flash of light, I shall see Him, but first He will come to me here.' Soon after he said, 'Why haven't they come? I am ready.' I said, 'The doctors will be here in a few minutes; had you not better wait till they are gone?' 'Oh, certainly, I should prefer waiting; I should not like them to break in on my thanksgiving.' When Mr. Tegart gave him some wine, he could not swallow it, and no doubt he saw that it was necessary for him to resign himself to the loss of Communion, for he did not speak of it again."

This same night he spoke to Reverend Mother about the glorious work that God was performing for

Ireland and England; that he was willing to stop to
work, but he did not see how it was possible for him
to recover; that God did not want any one, but could
make something better and brighter: and then something about the resurrection, but his memory refused
to supply him with the right words. Soon after, on
saying something the Reverend Mother could not
understand, he called Roper, and said to him, "Tell
Reverend Mother what I mean to say;" thinking no
doubt that one of them might guess his meaning.
After a pause, he said to her, "Have you been praying as I told you? Have you prayed that I may be
dissolved and be with Christ?" She answered, "I
have been praying for you—we always are." "Did
you pray," he said, "that I might go home? Do you
remember what I told you to say?" Thinking he
referred to what he had said on Thursday morning,
she said nothing in reply.

The Cardinal's own description of himself, before
he was reduced quite so low, was that he was like a
pendulum; and the doctors said that no comparison
could be more apt. Several times it seemed as if
death could not be far off; but each time he rallied,
though each time it was to a distinctly lower level of
strength.

On Wednesday night, a week before he died, the
medical men thought that he would not survive the
night, and then the prayers for the departing were
first said by Dr. Melia. They were repeated several
times afterwards. Early in the week he had asked

for the last blessing, and Monsignor Searle had given
it him; and by his wish it was repeated at intervals.

On Sunday the 12th he spoke three or four
times; but only a few words each time. That
morning Dr. Manning arrived, after a long and
fatiguing winter's journey from Rome. When he
first went into the Cardinal's room, he did not re-
cognise him at all. About half-an-hour later, to the
request, "Will you give Dr. Manning your blessing,
my Lord?" he answered, "Yes, when he comes."
When told "Here he is," he looked towards him and
stretched out his hand, which Dr. Manning, who
knelt beside him, placed upon his head, and then
said to him: "The Holy Father sends you his special
blessing, and bids me tell you of his great love for
you, especially at this point." The Cardinal said
three times, "I thank him;" and then, after a short
interval, "Thank him," also three times.

Soon after, while Mass was being said in his
ante-room, he turned to me and said, "Is not Mass
going on?"

He did not speak again before a quarter-past
seven in the evening, when he said to Reverend
Mother, "What is this great peace?" At the same
time he lifted his hand to the wound on his right
temple, when she said, "Don't touch it." He continued, "I don't mean the cut,—I mean of soul.
What is this great peace of soul? Where does it
come from?"

On one occasion Monsignor Searle asked him

whether he knew him; and his answer was, "I have never unknown you."

On the following day, Monsignor Thompson, one of the Cardinal's dearest friends, arrived. He entered the room very cautiously; but the Cardinal perceived that some one was there, and, when Monsignor Searle drew near him, he said, "I am to be kept quiet —quiet—quiet." And later on in the day he said to Roper, "Quiet, quiet." He only spoke once again this day. The light from the blessed candle that burned at the head of his bed pained his eye, and he said: "Blind me, blind me!"

At midnight, as I was standing beside him, I distinctly heard him pronounce my name. I instinctively answered, and he uttered a whole sentence, of which, to my great grief, I could not distinguish a single word. His mouth and tongue were so burnt and parched from the rapid passage of the dry hard breathing, that, except at rare intervals, he could not articulate.

At half-past two in the morning of Tuesday the 14th, Mr. Hawkins, who had him in his arms, assisting him to turn, heard him say: "The agony." There was probably an increase of difficulty in breathing, and though he was not immediately dying, we said, for his consolation, the prayers for the agonising. He raised his hand to shelter his eye from the light of a candle that pained him. At four o'clock he said to Reverend Mother, "I am going fast." At a quarter-past seven, he asked what o'clock

it was. At half-past seven, I said to him, "I am
going to say Mass for you—for a happy death. You
can hear it from where you are." He answered:
"Thank you: God bless you!"

 I do not know that he spoke again. Reverend
Mother thinks that she heard him say, during the
day, "My God, my God." This was his constant
ejaculation during his illness.

And now begins that portion of the past that I
need not recall. To be so powerless to help him was
the hardest of all to bear; painful as the previous
days of his utter weakness had been to those who
reverenced and loved him. Why should I dwell
upon these things now? For six-and-thirty hours,
and perhaps longer, he was gradually dying; and at
eight o'clock in the morning of Wednesday the 15th
of February, with the Church's words sounding in
his ears, as he had desired, he passed away to his
rest. The end was without a struggle. Calmly,
peacefully he departed. Monsignor Thompson and
Monsignor Manning had just said their Masses for
his happy death. After the prayer for a departed
soul, I offered the Holy Sacrifice for his repose ; and
my Mass was immediately followed by Monsignor
Searle's. He died in the midst of prayers and sacri-
fices.

"Constituat te Christus Filius Dei vivi intra
Paradisi sui semper amœna virentia, et inter oves
suas te verus ille Pastor agnoscat. Redemptorem
tuum facie ad faciem videas, et præsens semper

assistens, manifestissimam beatis oculis aspicias veritatem. Constitutus igitur inter agmina Beatorum, contemplationis divinæ dulcedine potiaris in sæcula sæculorum."

The following inscription was composed by the Cardinal in 1860 for a slab of marble to be laid in the choir of the Pro-Cathedral at Moorfields. A few days before his death he referred to it, requesting me to remind Dr. Gilbert to fill in the blank left for the date.

NICOLAVS · S · R · E · PR · CARD · WISEMAN

PRIMVS · ARCHIEPVS · WESTMONAST

NE · DE · MEMORIA · DEVM · PRECANTIVM

MERITO · EXCIDERET

HVNC · LAPIDEM · VIVVS · SIBI · POSVIT

QVI · CVM · AB · INEVNTE · ADOLESCENTIA

APVD · ANIMVM · SVVM · STATVISSET

IN · CHRISTIANA · RELIGIONE · VINDICANDA

IN : FIDE · CATHOLICA · ILLVSTRANDA

JVRIBVSQVE · ECCLESIAE · ET · S · S · TVENDIS

VITAM · INSVMERE · AB · HOC · PROPOSITO

VSQVE · AD · EXTREMVM · SPIRITVM

SCIENS · NVNQVAM · DECLINAVIT

A · SOLO · DEO · MERCEDEM · EXPECTANS

QVAM　　　·

AD · PEDES · INDVLGENTISSIMI · DOMINI · ROGATVRVS

DIEM · SVVM · OBIIT

[XV · FEBR · MDCCCLXV]

ORATE · PRO · EO